Temitope Ol

GRACEFUL ENCOUNTERS

STORIES OF NOTABLE PEOPLE IN THE BIBLE

PART 1

Graceful Encounters: Stories of Notable People in the Bible Part1
Copyright© 2024 Temitope Olorunfemi

All rights reserved.

No part of this publication may be reproduced, distributed, or transmitted in any form or by any means, including photocopying, recording, or other electronic or mechanical methods, without the prior written permission of the publisher except in the case of brief quotations embodied in reviews and certain other non-commercial uses permitted by copyright law.

Contact Author: booksbytemitope@gmail.com

Layout and Typeset Done by: Levi Digital Publishing

DEDICATION

Firstly I dedicate this book to God Almighty, the author and finisher of our faith, who has used the holy spirit to minister the idea to start this ministry on social media that has birthed this book.

To the memory of my beloved father, Mr. Ayodele Felix Olupeka, whose wisdom, love, and enduring spirit continue to inspire me every day. Though you are no longer with us, your legacy lives on in the values you instilled and the countless lives you touched.

And to my cherished mother, Mrs. Grace Yemisi Olupeka, whose unwavering faith, strength, and boundless love have been a guiding light in my life. Your resilience and grace have shown me the true meaning of dedication and devotion.

This book is dedicated to you, with all my love and gratitude.

CONTENT

Acknowledgement   7

Foreword   9

Introduction   11

Chapter One   14
THE STORY OF MARY THE MOTHER OF JESUS

Chapter Two   20
THE STORY OF JESUS CHRIST

Chapter Three   25
THE STORY OF RUTH AND BOAZ

Chapter Four   31
THE STORY OF ANANIAS AND SAPPHIRA

Chapter Five   37
THE STORY OF DEBORAH

Chapter Six   43
THE STORY OF ESTHER

Chapter Seven   49
THE STORY OF ABIMELECK

Chapter Eight   56
THE STORY OF SARAH

Chapter Nine   61
THE STORY OF HAGAR

Chapter Ten   66
THE STORY OF THE 10 VIRGINS

Chapter Eleven   71
THE STORY OF ANNA

Chapter Twelve   76
THE STORY OF RAHAB

Chapter Thirteen   80
THE STORY OF ELIJAH

Chapter Fourteen   84
THE STORY OF LOT

Chapter Fifteen   89
THE STORY OF SAUL

Chapter Sixteen   93
THE STORY OF JOB

Chapter Seventeen   98
THE STORY OF JOSEPH

Chapter Eighteen 103
THE STORY OF URIAH

Chapter Nineteen 108
THE STORY OF NOAH

Chapter Twenty 113
THE STORY OF DORCAS

Chapter Twenty-One 118
THE STORY OF CAIN AND ABEL

Chapter Twenty-Two 122
THE STORY OF SAMUEL

ACKNOWLEDGEMENT

I am deeply grateful to the many individuals who have supported and encouraged me throughout the journey of writing this book. Their contributions have been invaluable, and I am honoured to acknowledge them here.

First and foremost, I extend my heartfelt thanks to my beloved husband, Mr. Babatunde Olorunfemi. Your unwavering support, patience, and love have been my anchor throughout this process. Your insightful discussions and thoughtful feedback have enriched this work immeasurably. Thank you for believing in me and for being my constant source of strength.

I am profoundly grateful to my mentor, Pastor Temitope Olagbegi, whose wisdom and guidance have been instrumental in shaping this book. Your mentorship has been a beacon of light, providing clarity and direction at every stage. Your encouragement and constructive critique have challenged me to grow as a writer and thinker. Thank you for your steadfast support and for inspiring me to pursue this project with passion and dedication.

To my dear friends, Nnenna Sam-Obioha and Adesumbo Adeagbo, thank you for your unwavering friendship and encouragement. Your enthusiasm and belief in this book have been a constant source of motivation. The countless conversations, brainstorming sessions, and moments of laughter we shared have been a source of joy and inspiration. Your support has meant the world to me, and I am deeply grateful for your presence in my life.

This book is a testament to the collective support and encouragement of these extraordinary individuals. I am blessed to have each of you in my life, and I dedicate this work to you with profound gratitude.

FOREWORD

In a world where the roles and identities of men and women are continually evolving, the Bible stands as a timeless source of wisdom and insight. It offers a rich tapestry of narratives that highlight the complexities of human relationships, the dynamics of gender, and the profound interactions between the divine and humanity. This book, a deep dive into the lives of men and women in the Bible, offers readers a chance to explore these timeless stories with fresh eyes and thoughtful analysis.

From the creation stories of Genesis to the prophetic visions of Revelation, the Bible presents a diverse array of characters whose lives offer lessons and reflections that are still relevant today. This book does not merely recount their stories, it delves into the cultural, historical, and theological contexts that shaped their experiences and actions. It explores how their narratives illuminate broader themes of faith, power, and identity, providing a nuanced understanding of the biblical world.

The author skilfully brings to life the experiences of both prominent and lesser-known figures. We read about the patriarchs and matriarchs whose lives form the bedrock of biblical history, the judges and prophets who led and challenged Israel, and the apostles and disciples who spread the message of Christianity.

We also encounter the often overlooked but equally important stories of women like Deborah, Ruth, Esther, and Mary, whose faith and courage have inspired generations.

This book is not just an academic study, it is a journey through the Bible's portrayal of men and women, offering insights that are both profound and personal. It invites readers to reflect on their own lives and the ways in which these ancient stories speak to contemporary issues of humans and spirituality.

As you turn these pages, you will find a wealth of knowledge and inspiration. The author's meticulous research and heartfelt reflections provide a guide through the complex and beautiful narratives of the Bible. Whether you are a scholar, a believer, or someone seeking to understand the Bible's impact on gender and society, this book offers valuable insights and a deeper appreciation of the timeless truths within the sacred text.

It is my honour to introduce this compelling work, and I trust that it will enrich your understanding of the Bible and its enduring relevance to our lives today.

Sincerely,

Pastor Mrs Temitope Olagbegi.

INTRODUCTION

The Bible, an ancient and sacred text, is a tapestry of human experiences, divine interactions, and profound narratives that have shaped the spiritual and cultural foundations of countless generations. Among its many themes, the roles and representations of men and women stand out as pivotal elements that offer deep insights into the human condition and the divine plan.

From the creation accounts in Genesis to the prophetic visions of Revelation, the Bible presents a diverse array of characters whose lives and stories illuminate the complex interplay between gender, faith, and society. Adam and Eve, the first man and woman, set the stage for humanity's journey with God, their actions echoing through the ages in theological discourse and ethical reflection. The narrative of their lives, marked by disobedience and redemption, introduces fundamental questions about human nature, sin, and the promise of salvation.

As we traverse the pages of the Old Testament, we encounter patriarchs like Abraham, Isaac, and Jacob, whose stories are foundational to the identity of Israel. These men, chosen by God to lead and establish His covenant people, are portrayed with a mixture of faith, doubt, strength, and frailty. Alongside them are matriarchs such as Sarah, Rebekah, and Rachel, whose experiences of barrenness, motherhood, and familial strife highlight the significant yet often complex roles of women in the divine narrative.

The Old Testament also features remarkable women like Deborah, a prophetess and judge who led Israel to military victory and spiritual renewal; Ruth, a Moabite widow whose loyalty and love transcend cultural boundaries and bring about a lineage leading to King David; and Esther, whose bravery and intelligence save her people from annihilation. These women's stories, though ancient, resonate with timeless themes of courage, faith, and resilience.

Transitioning to the New Testament, we see the continued importance of both men and women in the unfolding of God's plan. Jesus Christ's interactions with women were revolutionary, affirming their worth and challenging societal norms. Women such as Mary, the mother of Jesus, Mary Magdalene, and the sisters Mary and Martha are depicted as integral to His ministry and the early Christian community. These narratives offer a countercultural perspective on gender roles, emphasizing the inclusivity of the Gospel message.

The apostles, particularly Peter and Paul, emerge as central figures in the spread of Christianity, their letters and acts forming a significant portion of the New Testament. Paul's epistles, while sometimes controversial in their directives regarding women, also include commendations of women leaders like Phoebe, Priscilla, and Junia, acknowledging their vital contributions to the early Church.

This book seeks to explore these biblical figures, examining how their lives reflect broader themes of gender, power, and divine purpose. Through careful analysis of the scriptural text and historical context, we aim to uncover the enduring lessons these ancient stories hold for contemporary readers, making it easy to understand and relate with. How did the cultural settings of the Bible shape the experiences of men and women? In what ways do these narratives continue to influence modern views on gender and spirituality?

By delving into the lives of these men and women, we will uncover a rich legacy of faith, courage, and resilience. Their stories offer not only a window into the past but also a mirror reflecting our ongoing journey towards understanding the divine and ourselves. As we engage with these texts, we invite readers to consider the dynamic interplay of tradition and transformation, challenge and affirmation, that characterizes the biblical portrayal of men and women. Through this exploration, we hope to provide a deeper appreciation of the Bible's complex and often surprising insights into the human experience.

Chapter One

THE STORY OF MARY THE MOTHER OF JESUS

Mary, also known as the Virgin Mary, plays a significant role in the Bible as the mother of Jesus Christ. According to the New Testament, Mary was a young Jewish woman who lived in Nazareth. She was betrothed to Joseph, a descendant of King David.

One day, the angel Gabriel appeared to Mary and announced that she had found favour with God. Gabriel told her that she would conceive by the power of the Holy Spirit and give birth to a son, whom she was to name Jesus. Despite her initial confusion, Mary humbly accepted this divine plan, saying, "I am the Lord's servant. May everything you have said about me come true."

Mary then visited her relative, Elizabeth, who was miraculously pregnant with John the Baptist. When Mary greeted Elizabeth, the baby leaped in Elizabeth's womb, and Elizabeth was filled with the Holy Spirit. Elizabeth blessed Mary, recognizing her as the mother of the Lord.

Mary returned to Nazareth and eventually married Joseph.

While Mary was pregnant, she and Joseph had to travel to Bethlehem for a census. They couldn't find a place to stay, so Jesus was born in a stable and placed in a manger. There, shepherds visited them after being informed by angels about the birth of the Messiah.

After Jesus' birth, Mary and Joseph later brought him to the temple in Jerusalem to present him to the Lord. While at the temple, they encountered Simeon, a devout man who had been waiting to see the Messiah. Simeon blessed Mary and prophesied that Jesus would bring salvation to both Jews and Gentiles.

Mary also played a part in Jesus' adult life and ministry. She witnessed his miracles, heard his teachings, and supported him throughout his public ministry. She was present at significant moments, including the wedding at Cana, where Jesus performed his first miracle of turning water into wine.

Perhaps one of the most poignant moments is Mary's presence at the crucifixion of Jesus. Standing at the foot of the cross, she witnessed her son's suffering and death. Jesus, in his final moments, entrusted Mary to the care of the apostle John, saying, "Here is your mother."

Following Jesus' resurrection and ascension, Mary, along with the other disciples, devoted herself to prayer. She is mentioned as being present with them in the upper room, waiting for the promised Holy Spirit, who would empower them for their mission.

Mary's life emphasizes her faith, humility, and willingness to trust in God's plan. She serves as an important figure in Christianity, revered for her role in bringing forth the Son of God.

KEY LESSONS LEARNED FROM THE STORY OF MARY

1. Faith and Trust: Mary's unwavering faith and trust in God are evident throughout her story. Even as a young woman facing an unexpected and miraculous pregnancy, she humbly accepted God's plan for her life. This teaches us the importance of having faith and trusting in God's purpose, even when faced with challenging circumstances.

2. Obedience to God's Will: Mary's response to the angel Gabriel demonstrates her obedience to God's will. Despite any personal concerns or societal challenges she might have faced, she willingly accepted her role in bringing Jesus into the world. This reminds us of the significance of obeying God's instructions, even when they may be difficult or go against societal expectations.

3. Humility and Servanthood: Mary's humble and servant-hearted attitude shines throughout her story. Instead of seeking glory or recognition for herself, she recognized herself as the Lord's servant and submitted to his plans. She consistently puts the needs of others above her own, such as when she cared for her young son and later stood at the foot of the cross during Jesus' crucifixion. This teaches us to cultivate humility and a willingness to serve others.

4. Motherly Love and Support: Mary's role as a mother highlights the importance of unconditional love, care, and support. She nurtured and cared for Jesus throughout his life, witnessing his ministry and remaining by his side even in his darkest moments. Mary's example reminds us of the significant impact that a loving and supportive mother can have on her children's lives.

5. Perseverance and Resilience: Mary faced various challenges and hardships throughout her journey, from the difficulties of being an unwed mother to the heart-wrenching experience of witnessing her son's crucifixion. However, she remained steadfast, resilient, and faithful until the end. Her story teaches us the importance of perseverance and resilience in the face of trials.

In conclusion the story of Mary the mother of Jesus serves as an inspiration and source of valuable lessons, highlighting faith, obedience, humility, love, and resilience. It encourages us to live lives that reflect these qualities and deepen our relationship with God.

NOTES

NOTES

Chapter Two

THE STORY OF JESUS CHRIST

The story of Jesus Christ, as chronicled in the New Testament of the Bible, begins with his birth in Bethlehem. According to the Gospels, he was born to the Virgin Mary through the Holy Spirit and was raised in Nazareth by his parents, Mary and Joseph.

As he reached adulthood, Jesus began his public ministry, gathering disciples and preaching about the coming of the Kingdom of God. He taught using parables, performed miracles such as healing the sick and raising the dead, and publicly challenged the religious authorities of the time.

Jesus teachings emphasized love, compassion, forgiveness, and the importance of inner purity. He drew large crowds and gained a following, but his message also sparked controversy and opposition from some religious leaders and Roman authorities due to its radical nature and perceived threat to the established order.

The pinnacle of Jesus story is his crucifixion and subsequent resurrection. He was betrayed by one of his disciples, Judas Iscariot, arrested, and condemned to death by crucifixion by the Roman governor Pontius Pilate. Following his crucifixion, he was buried in a tomb, and three days later, he rose from the dead, appearing to his disciples and others before ascending into heaven.

The story of Jesus Christ forms the foundation of Christianity and emphasizing his role as the saviour of humanity who offers redemption and eternal life. It has inspired countless works of art, literature, and music and continues to shape the lives of billions of people around the world.

KEY LESSONS LEARNED FROM THE STORY OF JESUS CHRIST

1. Love and Compassion: Jesus teachings emphasize love for others, including enemies, and the importance of showing compassion and empathy towards all people.

2. Forgiveness: Jesus example stresses the importance of forgiveness and reconciliation, teaching that individuals should forgive others as they themselves seek forgiveness.

3. Sacrifice and Redemption: The story of Jesus crucifixion and resurrection highlights the themes of sacrifice and redemption, demonstrating the belief in the atonement for humanity's sins.

4. Humility: Jesus life and teachings underscore the value of humility, encouraging individuals to serve others and to approach life with a spirit of humility and selflessness.

5. Faith and Hope: Jesus story encourages faith in God and instills a message of hope, promising the possibility of redemption and eternal life through faith and belief in his teachings.

These lessons encapsulate key aspects of the Christian faith and have continued to resonate with individuals across cultures and generations.

NOTES

NOTES

Chapter Three

THE STORY OF RUTH AND BOAZ

The story of Ruth and Boaz can be found in the Book of Ruth in the Bible. It is a beautiful tale of loyalty, love, and redemption.

The story begins during the time of the judges in ancient Israel when a famine struck the land. Elimelech, a man from Bethlehem, along with his wife Naomi and their two sons, moved to the country of Moab to find sustenance. While living in Moab, their sons married Moabite women named Orpah and Ruth.

Tragically, Elimelech died, and eventually, both of Naomi's sons died as well, leaving her a widow with her daughters-in-law. Hearing that the famine in Bethlehem had ended, Naomi decided to return home to her people. She encouraged her daughters-in-law to stay in Moab, but Ruth adamantly refused to leave Naomi's side. Ruth's words of loyalty and devotion became famous, as she declared, "Where you go I will go, and where you stay I will stay. Your people will be my people and your God my God."

So, Ruth and Naomi journeyed back to Bethlehem. Arriving there, they were both in dire circumstances with no male relatives to support them. Ruth chose to go out into the fields to glean after the harvesters, in order to gather enough food for them.

By divine providence, Ruth ended up gleaning in the fields owned by Boaz, a wealthy and respected man who was also a close relative of Naomi's deceased husband. Boaz noticed Ruth and was impressed by her hard work and her loyalty to Naomi. He showed her kindness and provided her with protection and abundant grain.

Naomi, recognizing Boaz's connection to their family, came up with a plan for Ruth's future. She instructed Ruth to go secretly to the threshing floor where Boaz would be sleeping after the harvest. Ruth followed Naomi's instructions, and in the middle of the night, she uncovered Boaz's feet and lay down at his feet. Surprised, Boaz woke up and found Ruth there, requesting that he "spread his garment" over her, symbolizing his willingness to marry her and provide protection and care.

Boaz was touched by Ruth's actions and agreed to marry her. However, there was a closer relative who had the right to marry Ruth based on custom. Boaz confronted the relative and informed him of the opportunity to marry Ruth and redeem the family's land. However, the relative declined the offer, giving Boaz the opportunity to marry Ruth.

In the end, Ruth and Boaz were married, and Ruth gave birth to a son named Obed. This child would become the grand-

grandfather of King David, making Ruth a significant figure in the lineage of Jesus Christ.

The story of Ruth and Boaz is not only a beautiful love story but also highlights important themes of loyalty, faithfulness, and God's providence in bringing about redemption and blessings in the lives of His people.

Boaz was touched by Ruth's actions and agreed to marry her. However, there was a closer relative who had the right to marry Ruth based on custom. Boaz confronted the relative and informed him of the opportunity to marry Ruth and redeem the family's land. However, the relative declined the offer, giving Boaz the opportunity to marry Ruth.

In the end, Ruth and Boaz were married, and Ruth gave birth to a son named Obed. This child would become the grandfather of King David, making Ruth a significant figure in the lineage of Jesus Christ.

The story of Ruth and Boaz is not only a beautiful love story but also highlights important themes of loyalty, faithfulness, and God's providence in bringing about redemption and blessings in the lives of His people

KEY LESSONS LEARNED FROM THE STORY OF RUTH AND BOAZ

1. Faithfulness: Ruth demonstrates unwavering faithfulness to her mother-in-law Naomi. Despite facing difficulties and being from a different culture, Ruth remains loyal and committed. This teaches us the importance of loyalty and faithfulness in our relationships.

2. Providence and God's Guidance: The story of Ruth showcases how God's providence and guidance can work behind the scenes. Ruth happens to glean in Boaz's field and this sets in motion a series of events that ultimately leads to their marriage. It reminds us that God can work through unexpected circumstances to bless and provide for us.

3. Redemption and Restoration: The relationship between Ruth and Boaz exemplifies the theme of redemption and restoration. Boaz, as the kinsman-redeemer, takes on the responsibility of marrying Ruth and restoring her name and inheritance. This highlights the concept of God's redemption and how He can bring restoration to our lives.

4. Kindness and Generosity: Boaz demonstrates kindness and generosity towards Ruth and Naomi. He not only allows Ruth to glean in his fields but also goes above and beyond by providing her with additional grain and protecting her. This teaches us the importance of being kind and generous to others, especially those in need.

These lessons from Ruth and Boaz's story have timeless relevance and can provide guidance in our relationships, faith, and daily lives.

NOTES

NOTES

Chapter Four

THE STORY OF ANANIAS AND SAPPHIRA

The story of Ananias and Sapphira is found in the New Testament of the Bible, specifically in the book of Acts, chapter 5, verses 1-11. It is a cautionary tale that highlights the importance of integrity and honesty.

Ananias and his wife Sapphira were members of the early Christian community in Jerusalem. During this time, many believers sold their possessions and willingly gave the proceeds to the apostles to distribute to those in need.

Ananias and Sapphira also decided to sell a piece of property, but they conspired to keep a portion of the money for themselves while appearing to give the full amount to the apostles. They made a deliberate choice to deceive both the apostles and the Holy Spirit.

Ananias went to the apostles and presented the money, claiming it was the full amount from the sale. However, Peter, one of the apostles, had been filled with the Holy Spirit and discerned Ananias' deceit. Peter confronted Ananias, questioning why he allowed Satan to fill his heart with lies.

Upon hearing Peter's words, Ananias immediately fell down and died. This sudden punishment shocked everyone who witnessed it. After a short period of time, Ananias' wife, Sapphira, arrived unaware of what had happened to her husband.

Peter questioned Sapphira, asking her if the amount they gave was the full price of the property. Just as her husband did, she lied and affirmed that it was the total amount. In response, Peter pronounced God's judgment on her, and Sapphira also fell down and died.

Their sudden deaths served as a powerful lesson to the early Christian community, emphasizing the importance of honesty, integrity, and sincerity in their actions and dealings within the community. The incident also demonstrated the seriousness of lying to the Holy Spirit.

The story of Ananias and Sapphira reminds believers of the importance of truthfulness and the need to align their actions with their professed faith. It serves as a warning against hypocrisy and dishonesty in the Christian community, encouraging believers to live with sincerity and integrity before God and others.

KEY LESSONS LEARNED FROM THE STORY OF ANANIAS AND SAPPHIRA

1. Honesty and Integrity: Ananias and Sapphira pretended to give all of the proceeds from the sale of their land to the community of believers but secretly kept back a portion for themselves. Their actions demonstrated a lack of honesty and integrity. The story warns us about the importance of being truthful in our in our dealings with others and maintaining integrity in our actions.

2. Hypocrisy: Ananias and Sapphira acted in a hypocritical manner by trying to deceive the early Christian community. They wanted to be seen as generous while holding back part of the profits. This teaches us the danger of hypocrisy and the importance of aligning our actions with our intentions.

3. God's Omniscience: The story of Ananias and Sapphira reminds us that God is all-knowing and sees the intentions of our hearts. Even though no human knew about their dishonesty, God revealed the truth to the apostle Peter. This illustrates that our actions may be hidden from others, but we cannot hide them from God.

4. Consequences of Deception: Ananias and Sapphira faced severe consequences for their dishonesty. Both of them died suddenly after being confronted by Peter about their deceit. This serves as a reminder that deceitful actions can have serious consequences, and we should be mindful of the choices we make.

5. Generosity and Sharing: The story of Ananias and Sapphira highlights the communal and generous spirit within the early Christian community. While their deceit was condemned, the underlying principle of selling possessions and sharing with those in need remains an important lesson for us today. It encourages us to be generous with our resources and consider the needs of others.

The story of Ananias and Sapphira serves as a cautionary tale about honesty, integrity, and the consequences of our actions. It teaches us to be genuine, truthful, and generous, while also reminding us that God sees and knows all.

NOTES

NOTES

Chapter Five

THE STORY OF DEBORAH

Deborah is a significant figure in the Bible, particularly in the Book of Judges. She was a prophetess and the only female judge mentioned in the Bible.

Deborah lived during a time when Israel was being oppressed by the Canaanites. The Israelites had done evil in the eyes of the Lord, so for 20 years they were under the cruel rule of King Jabin of Canaan and his commander, Sisera.

Deborah was not only a prophetess, but also a wise and respected leader. She held court under a palm tree between Ramah and Bethel in the hill country of Ephraim. The Israelites would come to her seeking guidance and resolution for their disputes.

At one point, Deborah received a message from God instructing her to call upon a man named Barak, from the tribe of Naphtali. She told Barak that God wanted him to gather an army of 10,000 men and confront Sisera. Barak was hesitant and asked Deborah to accompany him, saying that he would go only if she went with him.

Deborah agreed to go with Barak, but she warned him that because of his lack of faith, the honor of defeating Sisera would be given to a woman instead. Barak assembled his army, and they marched toward the enemy forces near Mount Tabor.

When Sisera learned of Barak's approach, he gathered his chariots and soldiers and attacked. However, God intervened and caused confusion among Sisera's troops. The Israelite army, led by Barak, was victorious.

Sisera, the commander of the Canaanite forces, managed to escape on foot and sought refuge in the tent of a woman named Jael. She lured him into a false sense of security and, while he slept, drove a tent peg through his temple, killing him.

After the battle, Deborah and Barak sang a victory song praising God for their triumph. The song, known as the Song of Deborah, is found in the Book of Judges and celebrates Israel's deliverance from their enemies.

Deborah's story reflects her courage, wisdom, and faithfulness to God. She served as a leader and judge during a challenging time for Israel, and her obedience to God's instructions ultimately led to their liberation. Her story continues to inspire people today, highlighting the importance of trusting in God and stepping out in faith.

KEY LESSONS LEARNED FROM DEBORAH'S STORY

1. Faithfulness: Deborah's unwavering faith in God is a key aspect of her story. Despite the challenging circumstances, she remained faithful and trusted in God's guidance. Her example reminds us of the importance of staying faithful to God even in difficult times.

2. Courage: Deborah demonstrated great courage by stepping into a leadership role during a time when women in such positions were uncommon. She didn't let societal norms hold her back and boldly followed God's call. Her story encourages us to have the courage to step out and lead, even when faced with opposition or uncertainty.

3. Wisdom and Discernment: Deborah's role as a judge involved providing wise counsel and resolving disputes among the Israelites. Her ability to hear from God and make sound judgments showcases the importance of seeking wisdom and discernment in our own decision-making processes.

4. Empowerment: Deborah's story is a testament to the empowerment of women. In a male-dominated society, she rose to prominence and led a successful military campaign. Her example challenges traditional gender roles and underscores the importance of recognizing and utilizing the gifts and abilities of both men and women.

5. Praise and Gratitude: After the victory over Sisera, Deborah and Barak sang a song of praise, known as the Song of

Deborah. It reflects their gratitude to God for the deliverance of Israel. This highlights the significance of expressing gratitude and praising God for His faithfulness in our own lives.

Deborah's story serves as an inspiration for faith, courage, wisdom, empowerment, and gratitude. Her example reminds us of the importance of trusting in God, stepping out in faith, and recognizing the potential within ourselves and others to bring about positive change.

NOTES

NOTES

Chapter Six

THE STORY OF ESTHER

The story of Esther in the Bible is a captivating tale from the Old Testament in Esther chapter 1-10. It showcases the bravery and resourcefulness of a Jewish woman named Esther, who became the queen of Persia and uses her position to save her people from a plot to exterminate them.

The story takes place during the reign of King Ahasuerus (also known as Xerxes I) in ancient Persia. The king throws a grand six-month-long banquet to showcase his riches. During the feast, he commands his queen, Queen Vashti, to appear before his guests, but she refuses. This angers the king, and he deposes Queen Vashti, seeking a new queen.

In search of a replacement, King Ahasuerus holds a beauty contest where women from across the kingdom are brought to the palace. Among them is Esther, an orphaned Jewish girl who is raised by her cousin Mordecai. Esther possesses remarkable beauty and catches the attention of the king, who chooses her to be his queen. However, Esther keeps her Jewish identity a secret at the advice of Mordecai.

Unknown to the king, his advisor Haman harbours a deep hatred for the Jews. When Mordecai refuses to bow down to him, Haman is filled with rage. Seeking revenge, Haman manipulates the king into issuing a decree to annihilate all the Jews in the kingdom on a specific day.

Upon learning of the plot, Mordecai urgently urges Esther to use her position as queen to intercede with the king and plead for the salvation of their people. However, approaching the king without being summoned is a risky and potentially deadly act. Mordecai reminds Esther that perhaps she has been uniquely positioned in the palace "for such a time as this."

Encouraged by his words, Esther decides to take action, saying, "If I perish, I perish." She fasts and prays for three days to seek God's help and guidance. Then, she boldly goes before the king, risking her life to plead for the lives of her people.

Esther approach the king and invites him and Haman to a banquet. During the banquet, Esther reveals her Jewish heritage to the king, expressing her concern for her people's impending doom. The king is shocked and furious, realizing the gravity of Haman's scheme. In a twist of fate, Haman is eventually executed on the very gallows he had intended for Mordecai.

The king grants Esther permission to issue a new decree allowing the Jews to defend themselves against their enemies. On the appointed day, the Jews successfully defend themselves and emerge victorious.

The festival of Purim is established to commemorate their

salvation, celebrating the courage of Esther and the deliverance of the Jewish people from destruction.

The story of Esther serves as an enduring testament to the power of courage, faith, and standing up for what is right, even in the face of great danger.

KEY LESSONS LEARNED FROM ESTHER'S STORY

1. **Courage and bravery:** Esther shows immense courage by risking her life to approach King Ahasuerus and plead for the salvation of her people. Her bravery serves as an inspiration for standing up for what is right, even when it is difficult or dangerous.

2. **Providence and divine timing:** The story emphasizes the idea of God's providence and how He orchestrates events for a purpose. Esther's position as queen is not a coincidence but a part of God's plan to save His people. It reminds us that God can use ordinary people in extraordinary ways.

3. **The power of prayer and fasting:** Before approaching the king, Esther calls for a three-day period of fasting and prayer. This highlights the importance of seeking God's guidance and intervention in times of adversity.

4. **The danger of hatred and discrimination:** The story reveals the consequences of Haman's hatred and prejudice towards the Jewish people. It reminds us of the destructive nature of hatred and discrimination and the importance of

treating others with respect and fairness.

5. God's faithfulness and deliverance: In the face of great danger, God remains faithful to His people. The story demonstrates how He turns the tables on their enemies and brings about deliverance, ultimately saving the Jewish people from destruction.

6. The importance of using one's influence for good: Esther's position as queen gives her a unique opportunity to use her influence to bring about positive change. Her story reminds us of the importance of using our own positions and abilities to advocate for justice and help those in need.

7. The significance of community and unity: Mordecai's role as Esther's supporter and advisor underscores the importance of community and unity. Together, they work towards a common goal, which leads to victory. It emphasizes the strength and support found in coming together as a community.

NOTES

NOTES

Chapter Seven

THE STORY OF ABIMELECK

The story of Abimelech is narrated in the book of Judges in the Bible. Abimelech was the illegitimate son of Gideon, who was a mighty judge and leader of Israel. After Gideon's death, Abimelech aspired to become king and rule over Israel. However, his quest for power and the lengths he went to achieve it ultimately led to his downfall.

Abimelech convinced the people of Shechem, where his mother was from, to support him in his desire to become their ruler. He claimed that it would be better for Shechem to have one ruler instead of relying on the sons of Gideon, whom he portrayed as incapable of ruling. The people of Shechem were convinced and gave Abimelech seventy pieces of silver from the temple of Baal-Berith to fund his campaign.

With this support, Abimelech hired worthless and reckless men as his followers. He then proceeded to his father's house in Ophrah and brutally killed his seventy half-brothers, except for Jotham, who managed to escape.

After eliminating his potential rivals, Abimelech was established as the ruler of Shechem. However, soon after,

Jotham appeared on Mount Gerizim and delivered a powerful parable to the people of Shechem, denouncing Abimelech's rule and prophesying his downfall. Jotham's words carried a curse pronouncing that fire would come out from Abimelech and devour the men of Shechem and vice versa.

While Abimelech maintained control for three years, a conflict arose between him and the men of Shechem. Gaal, the son of Ebed, led a rebellion and challenged Abimelech's leadership. This conflict escalated into a battle, with Gaal's forces eventually being defeated and forced into retreat.

Abimelech then turned his attention to the city of Shechem and set it on fire, killing many of its inhabitants. He then moved on to the nearby city of Thebez, but while besieging the city, a woman threw a millstone from the tower and crushed Abimelech's skull. Realizing the seriousness of his injury, Abimelech asked his armor-bearer to kill him, so he would not die at the hands of a woman. Abimelech's request was fulfilled, and he died.

Thus, Jotham's prophecy came to pass, as Abimelech and the people of Shechem both suffered the consequences of their actions. This marked the end of Abimelech's attempted reign as king and showed the futility of his pursuit of power through violence and deceit.

The story of Abimelech serves as a cautionary tale about the dangers of unchecked ambition, the consequences of forsaking God's plan, the destructive power of deceit, the responsibility of leadership, the importance of accountability, and the dangers of pride. It reminds us to seek God's guidance and align our aspirations with His will, upholding integrity and humility as we live our lives.

KEY LESSONS LEARNED FROM ABIMELECK

1. The dangers of unchecked ambition: Ambition in and of itself is not necessarily negative, but when it becomes unchecked and driven solely by self-interest, it can lead to disastrous outcomes. Abimelech's desire for power and kingship led him to commit abhorrent acts, including killing his seventy brothers in order to eliminate any potential threat to his authority. This serves as a cautionary tale about the dangers of ambition when not tempered by moral values.

2. The consequences of forsaking God's plan: Abimelech's actions were motivated by his desire to be king, even though it was not part of God's plan for Israel at that time. By disregarding God's will and seeking his own self-interest, Abimelech brought destruction upon himself and those around him. This reminds us of the importance of aligning our desires with God's plan for our lives, and acknowledging that our own will should never supersede His.

3. The destructive power of deception: Throughout the story, Abimelech exhibited a pattern of manipulation and deceit. He misled the people of Shechem into thinking he would be a just ruler and convinced them to support his claim to the throne. However, this deceit ultimately led to his downfall. The story highlights the destructive consequences of relying on deceit and manipulation, emphasizing the importance of honesty and integrity in our words and actions.

4. The importance of responsible leadership: Abimelech's rule was characterized by oppression and violence. Instead of acting as a just and righteous leader, he abused his power and brought harm to those under his authority. This reminds us of the crucial role that leaders have in society and the responsibility they bear to govern with wisdom, justice, and compassion. It is a reminder that leadership should be driven by selflessness and a desire to serve others rather than one's own interests.

5. The power of accountability: In Abimelech's story, we see the power of accountability at play. Though he was successful in consolidating power initially, his actions eventually caught up with him. God used Jotham, the only surviving brother, to pronounce a curse on Abimelech and the people of Shechem. This curse foreshadowed Abimelech's downfall and the ultimate justice that would be served. The story teaches us that individuals, no matter how powerful, are not above accountability. Eventually, our actions will have consequences, and justice will prevail.

6. The dangers of pride: Pride is a recurring theme throughout the story of Abimelech. His ambition and desire for power were fueled by his own pride. He saw himself as worthy of ruling over others and was willing to do anything to achieve that goal. However, his arrogance blinded him to the wisdom and guidance that could have been found in humility. Abimelech's story serves as a warning against the destructive nature of pride and the importance of cultivating humility in our own lives.

Overall, the story of Abimelech provides valuable lessons on the dangers of unchecked ambition, the consequences of forsaking God's plan, the destructive power of deceit, the responsibility of leadership, the importance of accountability, and the dangers of pride. By reflecting on these lessons, we can gain wisdom and apply them to our own lives, avoiding the pitfalls that Abimelech fell into and striving to live a life aligned with God's will and characterized by integrity and humility.

NOTES

NOTES

Chapter Eight

THE STORY OF SARAH

Sarah was also known as Sarai, is an important figure in the Bible. She plays a pivotal role in the story of Abraham and is commonly known as his wife. Here's an overview of her story:

Sarah's story begins in the book of Genesis in the Old Testament. She was the daughter of Terah and the wife of Abraham. However, when we first encounter her, she is unable to conceive a child.

God made a covenant with Abraham (then known as Abram) promising to bless him greatly and make him the father of many nations. But as the years went by and Sarah remained unable to conceive, doubts crept in.

Sarah, unable to bear children, suggested that her husband have a child with her maidservant, Hagar. Abraham followed this advice, and Hagar gave birth to a son named Ishmael. However, this arrangement caused discord within the family, as Sarah later became jealous of Hagar and Ishmael.

When Abraham was 99 years old and Sarah was 90, God appeared to Abraham and promised that he would have a child with Sarah. This miraculous news surprised Sarah, who overheard the conversation between Abraham and God and laughed in disbelief. Yet, true to God's promise, Sarah gave birth to a son and named him Isaac, which means "laughter."

Sarah's joy at becoming a mother was immense, and she became protective of her son. However, tensions escalated between Sarah and Hagar, resulting in Hagar and Ishmael being sent away. God promised to take care of them, and Ishmael went on to become the father of the Arab nations.

Sarah lived a long life, reaching the age of 127 before passing away. She was buried in the cave of Machpelah in Hebron, alongside Abraham.

Sarah's story teaches us about the power of faith, patience, and God's ability to fulfil his promises. She endured a long wait for her son, but ultimately her faith was rewarded, and she became the mother of Isaac, who played a significant role in the history of Israel.

KEY LESSONS LEARNED FROM SARAH'S STORY

1. Trust in God's promises: Sarah initially struggled to believe in God's promise of a child. However, her story demonstrates that despite doubts and challenges, trusting in God's faithfulness can lead to the fulfilment of His promises.

2. Patience and timing: Sarah's desire for a child was met with a long wait, Her story teaches us the importance of patience and understanding that God's timing may not align with our own, but His plans are always perfect.

3. Overcoming doubt: Sarah's laughter at the idea of having a child in her old age reflects her doubt. However, as her doubt transformed into faith, she experienced the blessing of motherhood. It reminds us that doubts and uncertainties can be overcome through trust and belief in God's power.

4. The power of perseverance: Despite facing difficulties and setbacks, Sarah never gave up hope. Her story is a testament to the power of perseverance and the rewards that can come when we persist in following God's plan.

5. Embracing God's calling: Sarah's role as a mother of nations highlights the importance of embracing God's calling on our lives. Her obedience and trust in God's guidance played a crucial role in shaping the future of the Hebrew people.

Sarah's story teaches us about faith, patience, trust in God's promises, and the strength that can come from overcoming doubt and embracing God's plan for our lives.

NOTES

NOTES

Chapter Nine

THE STORY OF HAGAR

The story of Hagar can be found in the Book of Genesis in the Bible. Hagar was an Egyptian slave and servant to Sarah, the wife of Abraham.

Sarah, who was unable to conceive a child, became impatient and offered Hagar to Abraham as a surrogate mother. Hagar became pregnant and tensions arose between her and Sarah. Sarah dealt harshly with Hagar, causing her to flee into the wilderness.

While Hagar was alone in the wilderness, an angel of the Lord appeared to her and instructed her to return to Sarah. The angel also promised Hagar that she would have a son named Ishmael, and that he would become the father of a great nation.

Hagar obeyed the angel and returned to Sarah, eventually giving birth to Ishmael. However, the relationship between Sarah and Hagar remained strained. When Sarah later bore her own son, Isaac, conflicts intensified.

Eventually, Sarah asked Abraham to send Hagar and Ishmael away. Although Abraham was initially hesitant, he received guidance from God to grant Sarah's request Hagar and Ishmael wandered in the desert once again, with minimal provisions.

In a moment of desperation, as their water supply ran out, Hagar left Ishmael under a shrub and distanced herself, unable to watch her son suffer. It was then that an angel of God appeared to Hagar, reassuring her that Ishmael would be protected and become a great nation.

Hagar's trust in God was renewed, and she discovered a well of water that saved both her and Ishmael from thirst. They settled in the desert of Paran, and Ishmael went on to father twelve sons, becoming the father of the Arab nations.

The story of Hagar illustrates themes of faith, hardship, and God's provision. It serves as a testament to God's care and guidance even in the midst of difficult circumstances.

LESSONS LEARNED FROM HAGAR'S STORY

1. Trust in God's Promises: Hagar's story reminds us of the importance of trust in God's promises. Even when faced with challenging situations, Hagar learned to trust that God would take care of her and her son. It serves as a reminder to have faith in God's plan for our lives and to trust in His provision.

2. God's Presence in our Wilderness: Hagar's encounter with the angel in the wilderness reveals that God is present even in our most isolated and desperate moments. It teaches us that even when we feel abandoned or alone, God is aware of our struggles and can provide comfort, guidance, and hope.

3. God's Care for the Vulnerable: Hagar's story highlights God's compassion and care for the vulnerable. As an Egyptian slave, Hagar was in a position of vulnerability, but God saw her affliction and intervened on her behalf. This encourages us to show compassion and care for those who may be marginalized or in need.

4. Embracing God's Plan: Hagar's experience demonstrated the importance of embracing God's plan, even when it may be different from what we initially desired or expected. Despite the difficulties she faced, Hagar accepted her role in God's plan and trusted His ultimate purpose.

5. A God Who Sees and Hears: Hagar named God "El-ROI," meaning "You are the God who sees me." Her encounter with God in the wilderness reminded her that God sees and hears the cries of his people, and He is attentive to our needs. It reassures us that God is aware of our struggles and is actively involved in our lives.

Hagar's story serves as a reminder of God's faithfulness, His presence in our lives, and the importance of trusting in His plans, even during challenging times.

NOTES

NOTES

Chapter Ten

THE STORY OF THE 10 VIRGINS

The story of the Ten Virgins is found in the New Testament of the Bible, specifically in the book of Matthew, chapter 25, verses 1-13.

Jesus tells a parable about ten virgins who took their lamps and went out to meet the bridegroom. Five of them were wise, and five were foolish. The wise virgins took extra oil for their lamps, while the foolish ones did not.

As they waited for the bridegroom to arrive, they all grew tired and fell asleep. At midnight, a cry was heard announcing the arrival of the bridegroom. The virgins woke up and began to trim their lamps.

The five foolish virgins quickly realized that their lamps were running out of oil, so they asked the wise virgins for some. However, the wise virgins refused, saying there might not be enough for all of them. They advised the foolish virgins to go and buy oil for themselves.

While the foolish virgins were away buying oil, the bridegroom arrived, and those who were ready went inside with him. The door was then shut. Later, the foolish virgins returned and knocked on the door, begging to be let in. However, the bridegroom replied that he didn't know them and refused them entry.

The parable concludes with Jesus' lesson: Watch therefore, for you know neither the day nor the hour in which the Son of Man is coming. The story symbolizes the importance of being spiritually prepared and vigilant, as we don't know when Jesus will return.

KEY LESSONS LEARNED FROM THE STORY OF THE 10 VIRGINS

1. Be prepared and watchful: The wise virgins who brought extra oil demonstrate the importance of being prepared and ready for whatever may come. They were vigilant and made sure they had enough oil for their lamps. Similarly, in our spiritual lives, we should be prepared for the coming of Jesus and remain watchful.

2. Spiritual readiness matters: The parable emphasizes the need for spiritual preparedness. The foolish virgins neglected to bring extra oil, portraying a lack of foresight and readiness. In our own lives, it is important to nurture our relationship with God, live out our faith, and be spiritually ready for Christ's return or any other challenges we may face.

3. Personal responsibility: Each person is responsible for their own spiritual preparedness. The wise virgins couldn't share their oil with the foolish ones, emphasizing that personal responsibility cannot be transferred. We are responsible for nurturing our faith, building a relationship with God, and seeking His Guidance individually

4. Time is limited: The parable highlights the unpredictable nature of the bridegroom's arrival, reminding us that life is fleeting and that we are unaware of when Jesus will return. It encourages us to prioritize our spiritual growth and not postpone it, as we have a limited amount of time to prepare.

5. There are consequences to irresponsibility: The parable highlights the consequences of being unprepared. The foolish virgins were shut out from the wedding feast because they were not ready. It reminds us of the importance of taking our faith seriously and not taking it for granted, as there may be consequences for neglecting our spiritual lives.

The parable calls us to be spiritually prepared, responsible, and vigilant in our relationship with God, reminding us to prioritize our faith and be ready for Christ's return or any other challenges we may encounter.

NOTES

NOTES

Chapter Eleven

THE STORY OF ANNA

Anna's story can be found in the book of Luke (Luke 2:36-38). She was a prophetess and a devout woman from the tribe of Asher. Anna was known for her dedication to God, spending her days in the temple, fasting, and praying.

She encountered Mary, Joseph, and the infant Jesus when they brought him to the temple for presentation according to Jewish law. Recognizing Jesus as the Messiah, she praised God and spoke about the child to all who were waiting for the redemption of Jerusalem.

Anna's story is brief in the Bible, but her faithfulness, devotion, and recognition of Jesus as the awaited Saviour are significant aspects of her narrative.

Anna's story in the Bible takes place during the time of Jesus' infancy. She was a widow for many years, having been married for only seven years before her husband passed away. Despite her widowhood, she devoted herself to a life of worship and service to God.

Living in Jerusalem, Anna spent much of her time in the temple, fasting, praying, and worshiping God. Her devotion and faithfulness were remarkable, and she was recognized as a prophetess, someone through whom God spoke.

When Mary and Joseph brought the infant Jesus to the temple to fulfil the customary rites of dedication and purification prescribed by Jewish law, Anna was present. As soon as she saw Jesus, she immediately recognized the significance of this child. She praised God and spoke about the child to all who were eagerly waiting for the redemption of Jerusalem, indicating to them that this infant was the long-awaited Messiah.

Anna's role in the Bible serves as a testament to the anticipation and recognition of Jesus as the fulfilment of Old Testament prophecies and the hope of salvation for the people of Israel. Her faithful dedication and proclamation of Jesus' significance contribute to the broader narrative of the birth of Christ.

LESSONS LEARNED FROM ANNA'S STORY

1. Dedication and Faithfulness: Anna's life exemplifies unwavering dedication and faithfulness to God. Her commitment to prayer, worship, and service in the temple, despite being a widow, demonstrates the importance of steadfast devotion to spiritual practices.

2. Recognition of the Messiah: Anna's immediate recognition of Jesus as the Messiah highlights the importance of spiritual discernment and insight. Her devotion allowed her to perceive the divine significance of Jesus' arrival, emphasizing the value of spiritual awareness and understanding.

3. Waiting with Hope: Anna, along with others, was waiting for the redemption of Jerusalem. Her story teaches the virtue of patient waiting with hope, trusting in God's promises even during times of waiting and uncertainty.

4. Proclamation of Truth: After recognizing Jesus, Anna shared the news with others eagerly waiting for redemption. Her boldness in proclaiming the truth about Jesus reflects the responsibility of sharing one's faith and experiences with others.

5. Role of Women in God's Plan: Anna, as a prophetess, occupies a significant place in the biblical narrative, showcasing the important role of women in God's plan and their ability to discern and proclaim divine truths.

Anna's story encourages us to cultivate dedication in our spiritual lives, seek understanding of divine truths, patiently wait for God's promises, boldly share our faith, and appreciate the vital role of women in religious contexts and society.

NOTES

NOTES

Chapter Twelve

THE STORY OF RAHAB

The story of Rahab is found in the book of Joshua, specifically in Joshua 2 and Joshua 6. Rahab was a woman living in the city of Jericho at the time when the Israelites, led by Joshua, were preparing to conquer the land of Canaan. Rahab is known as Rahab the Harlot and also known for her act of courage and faith in helping the Israelite spies.

When Joshua sent spies to Jericho to gather information, Rahab took them in and hid them from the king's men. In return for her help, she asked for protection for herself and her family when the Israelites attacked the city. The spies agreed, instructing her to tie a scarlet cord in the window of her house as a sign.

When Jericho fell, Rahab and her family were spared, as promised, and they became part of the Israelite community. Rahab is remembered for her bravery and her faith, and she is even mentioned in the New Testament in the book of Hebrews as an example of faith.

This story highlights the idea that God accepts and welcomes those who have faith in Him, regardless of their background or past. Rahab's story also demonstrates the power of God's mercy and the potential for redemption for all people

LESSONS LEARNED FROM THE STORY OF RAHAB

One of the key lessons is the power of faith and courage. Rehab, despite her background and circumstances, showed great faith and bravery in helping the Israelite spies and in trusting in the God of Israel. Her story also highlights the importance of compassion and kindness, as well as the idea that anyone, regardless of their past, can find redemption and a new beginning. Lastly, Rehab's story shows us that God's love and grace extend to all people, regardless of their background or past actions. These lessons remind us of the transformative power of faith and the possibility of redemption for everyone.

NOTES

NOTES

Chapter Thirteen

THE STORY OF ELIJAH

Elijah's story took place in the historical context of the divided kingdom of Israel. Who was featured in the books of 1 Kings and 2 Kings, and his ministry involved confronting the idolatry and unfaithfulness of the people of Israel and their rulers. One of the most well-known events is the showdown on Mount Carmel, where Elijah challenged the prophets of the false god Baal to a contest to see whose deity would answer with fire. Despite their best efforts, the prophets of Baal were unsuccessful, while the God of Israel gloriously demonstrated His power.

Elijah's story includes various encounters and struggles, such as his challenge to King Ahab's rule, his time of seclusion by the Brook Cherith, and his role in anointing Elisha as a prophet. Elijah had several encounters with Ahab and his wife, Jezebel, who were notably wicked rulers. He also experienced moments of doubt and fear, as well as instances of divine provision and miraculous intervention. Ultimately, Elijah's ministry serves as a testament to God's faithfulness and his power to work through his chosen servants, even in the face of significant opposition and adversity.

Additionally, Elijah is known for being taken up to heaven in a whirlwind, His story is both compelling and emblematic of God's presence and sovereignty in the lives of his people.

LESSONS LEARNED FROM THE STORY OF ELIJAH

1. It demonstrates the power of unwavering faith in God, even in the midst of difficult circumstances. Elijah's boldness and trust in God's provision, particularly during the showdown on Mount Carmel, showcase the importance of steadfast belief.

2. Elijah's moments of despair and discouragement following his encounter with Jezebel highlight the reality of emotional and spiritual struggles. His experience serves as a reminder of the importance of seeking God's presence and listening for His voice, especially during times of trial.

3. Elijah's eventual passing of his mantle to Elisha underscores the significance of mentorship and the transfer of wisdom and spiritual authority to the next generation. This illustrates the value of investing in and equipping future leaders.

The story of Elijah is a reminder of God's sovereignty, faithfulness, and provision, as well as the significance of standing boldly for the truth, even in the face of opposition.

NOTES

NOTES

Chapter Fourteen

THE STORY OF LOT

The story of Lot is found in the Book of Genesis 19:1-38. Lot was the nephew of the Abraham. Lot settled in the city of Sodom, which was known for its wickedness. When God decided to destroy Sodom and Gomorrah due to their sinfulness, two angels were sent to rescue Lot and his family. The angels warned Lot to escape the city and not to look back. Unfortunately, Lot's wife disobeyed and looked back, causing her to turn into a pillar of salt. Lot and his daughters survived and found refuge in a cave.

His story also highlights God's mercy and provision for those who remain faithful. Despite the impending judgment, the angels provided a way of escape for Lot and his family. Even though Lot's wife disobeyed and suffered the consequences, Lot himself and his daughters were spared due to their obedience and faith. This story is often used to illustrate themes of faith, judgment, and the importance of making choices that align with God's will.

LESSONS LEARNED FROM THE STORY OF LOT

It emphasizes the importance of making moral and spiritual choices, even when faced with worldly temptations. Lot's decision to dwell in Sodom, a city known for its wickedness, illustrates the potential consequences of aligning oneself with unrighteous. Additionally, the fate of Lot's wife serves as a reminder of the dangers of holding onto attachments that conflict with God's will and guidance.

Furthermore, the story of Lot underscores the importance of obedience and trust in God. Despite the impending judgment, God provided a means of escape for Lot and his family. This highlights the idea that, even in the face of adversity, God is merciful and provides a way for those who remain faithful and obedient to Him.

Lastly, the story encourages believers to prioritize spiritual values over material wealth and earthly pursuits. Lot's initial choice to settle in Sodom may have been motivated by a desire for prosperity, but the consequences of this decision were severe. This serves as a caution against the dangers of prioritizing material gain over spiritual well-being.

The story of Lot gives valuable insights into the importance of moral discernment, obedience to God's guidance, and the consequences of one's choices.

NOTES

NOTES

Chapter Fifteen

THE STORY OF SAUL

Saul, also known as King Saul, was the first king of Israel. His story is found in 1 Samuel and 2 Samuel. Saul was chosen as king by the prophet Samuel but later fell out of favour with God due to disobedience. He reigned for approximately 40 years.

Saul, later known as Paul, was a prominent figure in the Bible. Originally, he was a Pharisee and a zealous persecutor of early Christians. On his way to Damascus, he experienced a transformative encounter with a divine light and heard the voice of Jesus, leading to his conversion.

After this event, Saul became an ardent follower of Christ, adopting the name Paul. He played a crucial role in spreading Christianity, undertaking missionary journeys across the Roman Empire. Paul's letters, known as the Pauline Epistles, form a significant part of the New Testament, offering guidance to various Christian communities.

Saul's story includes his selection as king, his victories in battles against Israel's enemies, and his struggles with both internal and external threats. He famously clashed with a young David, who would eventually succeed him as king.

Saul's tragic downfall is a central part of his story. He sought to kill David out of jealousy and fear, eventually leading to his own death in battle, along with his sons.

Saul's story offers a complex portrayal of a leader chosen by God who struggled with his own insecurities, leading to tragic consequences. It serves as a cautionary tale about the dangers of pride, jealousy, and disobedience.

KEY LESSONS LEARNED FROM THE STORY OF SAUL

1. Transformative Power of Faith: Paul's life illustrates the profound impact that faith can have on an individual. His dramatic conversion on the road to Damascus shows that a sincere encounter with faith can lead to a radical transformation.

2. Forgiveness and Redemption: Paul's story exemplifies the concepts of forgiveness and redemption. Despite his past as a persecutor of Christians, he found forgiveness through his conversion and became a key figure in spreading the Christian message.

3. Courage in the Face of Adversity: Throughout his life, Paul faced numerous challenges, including persecution, imprisonment, and hardships during his missionary journeys. His resilience and courage teach us the importance of staying committed to one's beliefs even in difficult circumstances.

4. Inclusivity and Universality of Christianity: Paul played a crucial role in expanding Christianity beyond its Jewish roots. His teachings emphasized the inclusivity of the Christian message, reaching out to people from various backgrounds and cultures.

5. Purpose and Mission: Paul's life reflects a sense of purpose and a commitment to a mission. After his conversion, he dedicated his life to spreading the Gospel, undertaking extensive travels to share the message of Christianity.

6. Theological Contributions: Paul's letters, found in the New Testament, provide profound theological insights. His writings delve into topics like grace, faith, love, and the role of Christ in salvation, contributing significantly to Christian doctrine.

NOTES

NOTES

Chapter Sixteen

THE STORY OF JOB

The story of Job in the Bible, is found in the book of Job, it is one of great suffering, testing, and eventual restoration. Job was a wealthy man living in the land of Uz. He was known for his devotion to God and his righteous life. However, Satan believed that Job only served God because of the good things he had been given, so God allowed Satan to test Job's faith.

As a result, Job's wealth was taken from him, his children died, and he suffered from painful sores all over his body. Despite his suffering, Job refused to curse God. Instead, he questioned why he was suffering and sought understanding.

Job's friends attempted to comfort him, but they also questioned Job's integrity, believing that his suffering was a punishment for secret sins. However, Job maintained his innocence and demanded an audience with God to seek an explanation for his suffering.

Ultimately, God did appear to Job and spoke from a whirlwind. God questioned Job about the mysteries of the universe and Job's limitations as a human. Job realized his limitations and submitted to God's will, acknowledging that God's wisdom far exceeded his own.

In the end, God restored Job's prosperity, giving him twice as much wealth as before and blessing him with new children. The story of Job illustrates the importance of faith, perseverance, and ultimately, trusting in God's plan, even in the face of suffering and unanswered questions.

KEY LESSONS LEARNED FROM THE STORY OF JOB

1. Perseverance and faith: Job's steadfast faith, even in the midst of immense suffering, teaches the importance of holding onto one's faith during difficult times.

2. Trusting in God's wisdom: Job's ultimate realization of his own limitations and God's limitless wisdom highlights the importance of trusting in a higher power even when we don't understand the reasons behind our suffering.

3. The limitations of human understanding: Job's encounter with God emphasizes the fact that humans may not always understand the larger plan or reasons behind their suffering. It encourages humility and acceptance of our limited perspective.

4. Compassion and support: Job's friends, while imperfect in their approach, demonstrate the importance of offering compassion and support to those who are suffering, even if we may not fully understand their situation.

5. Restoration and hope: The story's conclusion, with job's restoration and blessing, offers hope and a reminder that suffering is not the end. It illustrates that there can be light at the end of the tunnel and that restoration is possible after hardship.

The story of Job provides profound insights into the nature of suffering, faith, and the human experience, offering lessons that resonate across different cultures and belief systems.

NOTES

NOTES

Chapter Seventeen

THE STORY OF JOSEPH

The story of Joseph is found in the Book of Genesis(37-50) in the Bible. Joseph was the favoured son of his father, Jacob, and he was given a coat of many colours, which made his brothers jealous. Their envy led them to sell Joseph into slavery, and he was taken to Egypt.

In Egypt, Joseph ended up serving in the household of Potiphar, an officer of Pharaoh. However, he was falsely accused by Potiphar's wife and thrown into prison. Through a series of events, Joseph gained a reputation for interpreting dreams, which ultimately led him to be called upon to interpret Pharaoh's dreams.

Joseph's interpretation of Pharaoh's dreams, which prophesied seven years of plenty followed by seven years of famine, led to him being elevated to the position of vizier, the highest-ranking official in Egypt, just below Pharaoh. As vizier, Joseph wisely managed the food supplies during the years of plenty, which ensured that Egypt was prepared for the famine.

Meanwhile, the famine also affected Canaan, where Joseph's family resided. Jacob sent his sons to Egypt to buy grain, where they encountered Joseph, although they did not recognize him. Eventually, Joseph revealed his identity to them, and he brought his entire family to Egypt, where Pharaoh welcomed them and provided for them.

The story of Joseph is a remarkable tale of faith, forgiveness, and redemption. Despite facing numerous hardships and betrayals, Joseph remained steadfast in his belief in God, and he ultimately used his position to save his family and many others from starvation.

This story has been cherished for generations for its enduring themes of resilience, forgiveness, and the belief that even in the darkest of times, there is hope and the possibility of redemption.

KEY LESSONS LEARNED FROM JOSEPH'S STORY

1. The power of forgiveness: Joseph forgave his brothers for selling him into slavery, despite the pain and suffering they caused him. This act of forgiveness allowed for healing and reconciliation within his family.

2. Faithfulness and integrity: Throughout his trials, Joseph remained faithful to his beliefs and maintained his integrity. This unwavering faith ultimately led to his rise to power and his ability to help others.

3. God's providence: The story of Joseph demonstrates that even in times of hardship and adversity, God's plan can ultimately lead to good outcomes. Joseph's experiences serve as a reminder that challenges can present opportunities for growth and ultimately lead to positive outcomes.

4. Perseverance: Despite enduring slavery, false accusations, and imprisonment, Joseph remained resilient and persevered through his circumstances. His perseverance ultimately led to his ascension to a position of great influence and the ability to help many people.

5.The importance of family: The reconciliation between Joseph and his brothers underscores the significance of family and the power of healing and restoration within familial relationships.

The story of Joseph gives insight into the value of forgiveness, the rewards of perseverance, the role of faith in difficult times, and the influential impact one person's actions can have on those around them. These valuable lessons continue to inspire and resonate with people from all walks of life.

NOTES

NOTES

Chapter Eighteen

THE STORY OF URIAH

Uriah story is found in the Book of 2Samuel 12, He was a Hittite and a loyal soldier in King David's army. The most notable account involving Uriah is related to David's affair with Bathsheba.

While David was king, he spotted Bathsheba, the wife of Uriah, bathing on a rooftop. Despite knowing she was married, David succumbed to temptation and committed adultery with her. When Bathsheba informed David that she was pregnant, he attempted to conceal the affair by bringing Uriah back from the battlefield and encouraging him to spend time with his wife.

However, Uriah's unwavering loyalty to his fellow soldiers and commitment to duty led him to refuse the comforts of home while his comrades were still at war. Frustrated by Uriah's integrity, David devised a plan to cover up his transgression. He ordered Uriah to be placed in a vulnerable position on the battlefield, ensuring his death.

Uriah indeed perished in battle, and after a period of mourning, Bathsheba became David's wife. The prophet Nathan later confronted David about his actions, leading to repentance. Uriah's story serves as a tragic narrative of loyalty, betrayal, and the consequences of David's moral failure.

LESSONS LEARNED FROM URIAH'S STORY

1. Loyalty and Integrity: Uriah's unwavering commitment to his duty and comrades, even at the expense of personal comfort, highlights the virtue of loyalty and integrity.

2. Abuse of Power: King David's abuse of power, succumbing to temptation, and orchestrating Uriah's death reflects the dangers of using authority for personal gain and the ethical implications of such actions.

3. Consequences of Sin: The story underscores the idea that even powerful individuals are not exempt from the consequences of their actions. David faced severe repercussions, including the death of his child and ongoing challenges within his family.

4. Repentance and Forgiveness: Despite David's grave sins, his repentance and acknowledgment of wrongdoing serve as a reminder that genuine remorse and seeking forgiveness can lead to redemption.

5. Human Frailty: The narrative emphasizes the frailty of human nature and the capacity for even respected figures to make grievous mistakes. It encourages humility and recognition of one's vulnerabilities.

6.Importance of Accountability: The role of the prophet Nathan in confronting David illustrates the importance of accountability. Having someone who holds individuals accountable for their actions is crucial in promoting righteousness.

Uriah's story serves as a cautionary tale about the consequences of unethical behaviour, the value of loyalty and integrity, and the potential for redemption through repentance.

NOTES

NOTES

Chapter Nineteen

THE STORY OF NOAH

The story of Noah is found in the Book of Genesis in the Bible, it's a well-known account of God's judgment and mercy.

Noah was a righteous man who lived during a time when the Earth was filled with wickedness and corruption. God saw the evil in the world and decided to bring a great flood to cleanse the Earth of all living creatures. However, because of Noah's righteousness, God chose him to build an ark to save his family and pairs of every kind of animal from the impending flood.

God gave Noah specific instructions on how to build the ark, including its size, dimensions, and materials. Noah followed these instructions faithfully, working on the ark for many years. As the ark neared completion, Noah gathered his family and the animals and entered the ark.

After they were safely inside, the floodwaters began to cover the Earth. It rained for forty days and forty nights, and the waters rose so high that even the tallest mountains were covered. All living things outside the ark perished in the flood.

For many days, Noah and his family floated on the ark, waiting for the waters to recede. Eventually, the ark came to rest on the mountains of Ararat, and Noah sent out a raven and a dove to find dry land. When the dove returned with an olive leaf, Noah knew that the waters had receded enough for them to leave the ark.

Noah, his family, and the animals disembarked from the ark, and God made a covenant with Noah, promising never to destroy the Earth again with a flood. As a sign of this covenant, God placed a rainbow in the sky as a symbol of His promise.

KEY LESSONS LEARNED FROM NOAH'S STORY

1. Obedience and faith
Noah's obedience to God's command to build the ark, despite the ridicule and disbelief of others, demonstrates the importance of obedience and faith in following God's directions, even when they may seem challenging or unconventional.

2. God's mercy and provision
The story of Noah illustrates God's mercy and provision for His people. Despite the wickedness and corruption on Earth, God chose to save Noah and his family, along with pairs of every kind of animal, from the great flood. This shows God's care and protection for those who are faithful to Him.

3. Preparation and diligence

Noah spent many years diligently working on building the ark according to God's instructions. This teaches us the importance of being prepared and diligent in our work, even when it may require patience and perseverance.

4. Covenant and promise

After the flood, God made a covenant with Noah and all living creatures, promising never to destroy the Earth with a flood again. This covenant signifies God's faithfulness and serves as a reminder of His promises to His people.

5. Restoration and new beginnings

The flood served as a means of cleansing and restoration for the Earth. The story of Noah's ark symbolizes new beginnings and the opportunity for renewal and restoration after difficult times.

6. God's sovereignty and judgment

The story of Noah also highlights God's sovereignty and ability to judge the actions of humanity. It serves as a warning about the consequences of sin and disobedience, while also showcasing God's ultimate authority.

The story of Noah and the Ark offers lessons on obedience, faith, God's mercy, preparation, covenant, restoration, and God's judgment. It continues to be a powerful and timeless narrative that speaks to themes of trust in God, redemption, and the hope of new beginnings.

NOTES

NOTES

Chapter Twenty

THE STORY OF DORCAS

Dorcas, also known as Tabitha, whose story specifically mentioned in the Book of Acts, chapter 9, verses 36-43.

Dorcas was a disciple who lived in the town of Joppa, located on the coast of the Mediterranean Sea. She was known for her acts of kindness and charity, particularly for making garments for the widows in her community. One day, Dorcas became ill and died. Her fellow believers in Joppa were deeply saddened by her passing and prepared her body for burial.

Meanwhile, in the nearby town of Lydda, the apostle Peter was visiting and performing miracles in the name of Jesus Christ. Upon hearing of Dorcas's death, some of the believers from Joppa sent for Peter, hoping that he could do something miraculous. Peter arrived in Joppa and was taken to the upper room where Dorcas's body lay. After praying, Peter turned to the body and said, "Tabitha, get up." Miraculously, Dorcas opened her eyes, sat up, and Peter helped her to her feet.

The news of Dorcas's resurrection spread quickly throughout Joppa, and many people came to believe in the Lord because of this miraculous event. Dorcas's story illustrates the power of faith and the compassion of believers in the early Christian community. She is remembered for her acts of kindness and the miracle of her resurrection, which brought glory to God and strengthened the faith of those who witnessed it.

KEY LESSONS LEARNED FROM THE STORY OF DORCAS

1. Compassion and Generosity: Dorcas is remembered for her acts of kindness and charity, particularly for making garments for widows. Her life teaches us the importance of showing compassion and generosity towards others, especially those in need. Community and Support: Dorcas was deeply valued by her community in Joppa. Her death brought great sorrow to those who knew her. This highlights the significance of community and support networks in times of loss and hardship.

2. Faith and Miracles: The story of Dorcas's resurrection through the intervention of the apostle Peter underscores the power of faith and the possibility of miracles. It reminds us that with God, all things are possible, and miracles can occur even in the midst of despair.

3. Service and Ministry: Dorcas's life of service and ministry to others exemplifies the Christian call to love one another and serve those in need. Her actions demonstrate the profound impact that one person can have on their community through acts of service and kindness.

4. Belief in Christ's Resurrection: Dorcas's resurrection serves as a powerful testament to the reality of Christ's resurrection and the hope of eternal life for believers. It reaffirms the Christian belief in life after death and the promise of resurrection for those who have faith in Christ. Overall, Dorcas's story inspires us to live lives characterized by compassion, generosity, and faith, as we seek to serve others and bring glory to God in all that we do.

NOTES

NOTES

Chapter Twenty-One

THE STORY OF CAIN AND ABEL

The story of Cain and Abel is not only a narrative of sibling rivalry but also a profound exploration of human nature and the consequences of our actions.

Cain's jealousy towards Abel stemmed from a feeling of inadequacy and a sense of unfairness in God's preference for Abel's offering. Despite both brothers making offerings to God, Cain's heart was not in his sacrifice as much as Abel's was. Cain's resentment towards Abel grew into envy, leading him to commit the ultimate sin of murder.

The story highlights the destructive power of envy and unchecked emotions. Cain's jealousy blinded him to reason and empathy, ultimately resulting in a tragic outcome. It serves as a warning about the dangers of harbouring negative emotions and the importance of managing them constructively.

Moreover, Cain's response to God's inquiry "Am I my brother's keeper"? illustrates a lack of responsibility and accountability for one's actions. It reflects a mindset of denial and avoidance of moral responsibility, which further deepens Cain's guilt and alienation from God.

God's punishment of Cain with banishment and marking him so that no one would harm him underscores the severity of his crime and the divine justice at play. Despite his wrongdoing, God still shows mercy towards Cain by sparing his life, albeit with consequences.

The story of Cain and Abel serves as a timeless lesson about the power of emotions, the importance of moral responsibility, and the consequences of our choices. It invites reflection on our own attitudes and behaviours towards others, urging us to strive for peace, empathy, and righteousness in our interactions.

KEY LESSONS LEARNED FROM CAIN AND ABEL'S STORY

1. Jealousy and its Consequences: The story warns about the destructive nature of jealousy, as Cain's envy led him to commit a grave sin.

2. Accountability for Actions: Cain faced consequences for his actions, highlighting the importance of being accountable for one's deeds.

3. Sibling Relationships: Cain and Abel's story sheds light on the complexities of sibling relationships, cautioning against negative emotions and actions within families.

4. The consequences of sinful behaviour and the importance of choosing virtuous paths.

5. The significance of seeking forgiveness and reconciliation rather than succumbing to hatred and violence.

NOTES

NOTES

Chapter Twenty-Two

THE STORY OF SAMUEL

The story of Samuel in the Bible is found primarily in the Old Testament, in the books of 1 Samuel and 2 Samuel. Samuel was a significant figure in ancient Israel, serving as a prophet, priest, and judge.

Samuel's story begins with his miraculous birth. His mother, Hannah, was barren and prayed fervently to God for a child. In answer to her prayers, she conceived and bore Samuel. In gratitude, Hannah dedicated Samuel to serve God from a young age, so she brought him to the house of Eli, the priest at the tabernacle in Shiloh.

As a boy, Samuel ministered in the tabernacle under Eli's guidance. One night, Samuel heard a voice calling his name and, thinking it was Eli, went to him. However, Eli realized it was God who was calling Samuel, so he instructed Samuel to respond, "Speak, Lord, for your servant is listening." This marked the beginning of Samuel's prophetic calling.

Throughout his life, Samuel served as a faithful prophet of God, delivering messages and guidance to the people of Israel. He played a crucial role in the transition from the period of the judges to the monarchy in Israel.

At the request of the people, Samuel anointed Saul as the first king of Israel. However, Saul's disobedience to God led to Samuel's later anointing of David as king, marking the beginning of David's rise to power.

Samuel continued to serve as a prophet and advisor to both Saul and David, delivering messages from God and providing guidance during times of crisis. He played a pivotal role in shaping the destiny of Israel and maintaining the nation's covenant relationship with God.

Samuel's life and ministry exemplify faithfulness, obedience, and dedication to God's call. He remained a steadfast servant of God throughout his life, leaving behind a legacy of wisdom and leadership for future generations.

KEY LESSONS LEARNED FROM SAMUEL'S STORY

1. Faithfulness and Perseverance in Prayer: Samuel's mother, Hannah, exemplifies persistence in prayer and faithfulness to God. Her earnest prayers for a child were answered, demonstrating the power of steadfast faith and dedication in seeking God's help.

2. Listening to God's Voice: Samuel's response to God's call, "Speak, Lord, for your servant is listening," teaches the importance of attentiveness to God's voice and readiness to heed His guidance. It underscores the significance of cultivating a receptive heart to discern God's will.

3. Servanthood and Obedience: Samuel's willingness to serve God from a young age, even under the tutelage of Eli, highlights the importance of humility, obedience, and readiness to fulfil God-given tasks, regardless of one's age or status.

4. Leadership with Integrity: As a prophet and judge, Samuel displayed integrity, impartiality, and righteousness in his leadership. His commitment to upholding God's laws and delivering justice serves as a model for leaders today, emphasizing the importance of moral integrity and adherence to God's principles.

NOTES

NOTES

Printed in Great Britain
by Amazon

45054890R00078